# The Unleashed Advertiser: Mastering Explosive Sales Techniques

I0845277

## CHAPTERS

### Introduction:

- Marketing is more than just selling products; it's about connecting with customers on a deeper level. In this ebook, we'll explore the art of understanding consumer psychology to create powerful marketing campaigns.
- As markets evolve, we need to adapt our strategies. We'll dive into the concept of market sophistication and how it influences advertising effectiveness.
- Get ready to embark on a journey that will transform the way you approach marketing and help you build stronger connections with your target audience.

### Chapter 1: The Journey of Market Awareness

- In this chapter, we'll explore the five stages of market awareness: from customers being totally unaware of their problem to being fully aware of your product as the solution.
- Understanding each stage will help you tailor your marketing messages and promotions to meet the specific needs of your potential customers at different points in their buying journey.
- We'll examine real-life examples of successful marketing campaigns that have effectively addressed each stage of market sophistication.

### Chapter 2: Building Emotional Connections

- Emotions are the heart of consumer behavior. In this chapter, we'll discover how to tap into the emotions of your target audience to create strong connections.
- By identifying and addressing the intense desires, fears, and frustrations of your customers, you can create marketing messages that truly resonate with them.
- We'll explore the use of storytelling, powerful visuals, and relatable characters to evoke emotions that inspire action and loyalty.

### Chapter 3: The Special Ingredient: Unique Selling Proposition (USP)

- Your Unique Selling Proposition (USP) sets you apart from competitors. We'll dive into the process of creating a compelling USP that speaks directly to your target audience's needs and wants.
- Together, we'll craft a clear and memorable USP that communicates the unique benefits of your product or service, leaving a lasting impression on your customers.
- Real-world case studies will illustrate how businesses have leveraged their USPs to achieve marketing success.

### Chapter 4: Unleashing Creative Brilliance: "The Big Idea"

- In this chapter, we'll explore the power of "The Big Idea" and how it can elevate your marketing campaigns to new heights.

- We'll guide you through brainstorming and refining your creative ideas to craft a message that captivates your audience and leaves a lasting impact.
- Drawing inspiration from iconic marketing campaigns, we'll see how a compelling "Big Idea" can be a game-changer for your business.

## Chapter 5: Crafting Compelling Copy

- Words have the power to move hearts and minds. This chapter will focus on honing your copywriting skills to create persuasive and engaging marketing materials.
- From attention-grabbing headlines to compelling body copy, we'll explore the essential elements of persuasive writing.
- Through practical exercises, you'll gain hands-on experience in crafting copy that connects with your audience and drives action.

## Chapter 6: Connecting with Your Audience

- Building a meaningful connection with your audience is key to successful marketing. We'll go beyond demographics to understand the psychographics and motivations of your target customers.
- By empathising with your audience's values and aspirations, you'll develop marketing messages that truly resonate with them.
- We'll discuss various segmentation strategies to ensure that your messages reach the right people at the right time.

## Chapter 7: Testing and Measuring Your Success

- Effective marketing requires continuous improvement. In this chapter, we'll dive into the importance of testing and measuring the performance of your marketing campaigns.
- From A/B testing to tracking key performance indicators (KPIs), we'll equip you with the tools to evaluate your marketing efforts effectively.
- Data-driven insights will help you optimize your campaigns, boost ROI, and make informed decisions for future marketing initiatives.

## Chapter 8: The Power of Education in Marketing

- Educating your audience can be a powerful marketing strategy. We'll explore how providing valuable information builds trust and establishes your authority in the industry.
- Through educational content marketing, you'll position your brand as a go-to resource, fostering long-term relationships with customers.
- We'll discuss content formats such as blog posts, guides, and videos to deliver informative content that engages and empowers your audience.

## Chapter 9: Unveiling Market Insights through Research

- Market research is the backbone of successful marketing strategies. This chapter will guide you through various research methods to gain valuable insights into your target market.
- We'll cover customer surveys, focus groups, competitor analysis, and other techniques to help you uncover trends, preferences, and pain points in your industry.
- Armed with data-driven insights, you'll make informed decisions and tailor your marketing efforts for maximum impact.

## Chapter 10: The 80/20 Rule: Maximising Marketing Impact

- The Pareto Principle, or the 80/20 rule, is a powerful concept that can transform your marketing efforts. We'll explore how to identify the most impactful 20% of your marketing activities that drive 80% of your results.
- By focusing on what works best, you'll optimise your marketing budget and resources for maximum return on investment.
- Real-life examples will illustrate how businesses have embraced the 80/20 rule to achieve outstanding marketing success.

## Conclusion:

- Congratulations! You've completed an enriching journey through the heart of marketing.
- Embrace your newfound knowledge and approach marketing with a fresh perspective.
- Remember, marketing is a dynamic field, and continuous learning and adaptation are the keys to sustained success. Keep exploring, experimenting, and connecting with your audience to build stronger and more meaningful relationships. Happy marketing!

# INTRODUCTION

**"The Unleashed Advertiser: Mastering Explosive Sales Techniques"** is your essential guide to thriving in the competitive world of online advertising. If you're an online advertiser facing challenges in selling products and services, this ebook provides powerful strategies and techniques to connect deeply with your audience.

The journey begins with understanding "market sophistication" and how different stages of consumer awareness impact your advertising. You'll learn to tailor messages to meet your audience's evolving needs effectively.

Emotions play a significant role in driving consumer behaviour. Discover how to create marketing messages that resonate with desires, fears, and frustrations, forging genuine connections with your audience.

Craft a compelling Unique Selling Proposition (USP) that sets your brand apart from competitors, showcasing your distinct value to potential customers.
Unleash your creative brilliance with "The Big Idea," captivating audiences and compelling them to take action.

Master effective copywriting to create persuasive messages that convert prospects into loyal customers.
Connect with your audience on a personal level, going beyond demographics to understand psychographics and motivations.
Optimise your marketing efforts through testing, measuring, and data analysis.
Educate your audience to build trust and authority in your industry.

Unveil valuable market insights through research, refining your strategies to meet customer needs.
Embrace the 80/20 rule to maximize your marketing impact, focusing on what truly drives results.
Get ready to unleash your online success and revolutionise your marketing approach. Happy reading and even happier marketing!

## Chapter 1: The Journey of Market Awareness

In the fast-paced world of online marketing, understanding your target audience is the first step toward success. This chapter will take you on a journey through the five stages of market awareness, illuminating the significance of adapting your marketing messages to meet your audience's needs at each stage.

**1.1** Understanding Market Sophistication As markets evolve, consumers become more sophisticated in their decision-making. The five stages of market awareness are:

- Stage 1: Totally Unaware - Customers are oblivious to their problem and the potential solutions.
- Stage 2: Problem-Aware - Consumers recognize they have a problem but aren't yet aware of specific solutions.
- Stage 3: Solution-Aware - Customers are aware of potential solutions but haven't decided on a particular product or service.
- Stage 4: Product-Aware - Consumers know about your product or service, but they may be hesitant to make a decision.
- Stage 5: Most Aware - Customers are well-informed and ready to make a purchase decision.

**1.2** Tailoring Messages for Each Stage Once you grasp the different stages of market awareness, you can tailor your marketing messages to match your audience's current level of sophistication. By doing so, you'll effectively communicate the value of your offerings and guide them through their buying journey.

For Stage 1, focus on raising awareness of the problem and its implications. Create content that grabs attention and sparks curiosity, drawing customers into the next stages.

For Stage 2, position your brand as a potential solution and educate consumers about the available options. Showcase the benefits of solving the problem and address common concerns.

At Stage 3, emphasize how your product or service stands out among the solutions. Provide clear differentiators and demonstrate why you're the best choice.

In Stage 4, build trust and credibility by addressing specific objections and providing social proof through testimonials and case studies.

Finally, at Stage 5, focus on closing the sale by offering discounts, limited-time promotions, or guarantees to encourage immediate action.

1.3 Real-Life Examples To reinforce the concepts, we'll examine real-life examples of successful marketing campaigns that effectively address different stages of market awareness. These case studies will showcase how companies strategically tailor their messages to captivate their audience and drive them toward making a purchase.

By understanding the journey of market awareness and applying these principles to your marketing strategy, you'll gain a competitive edge and maximize your chances of converting prospects into loyal customers. Get ready to navigate the stages of market sophistication and unlock the potential of your online marketing efforts.

1.4 Monitoring and Adapting As you progress through your marketing campaigns, it's essential to monitor their performance and customer feedback. Keep a close eye on key performance indicators (KPIs) to gauge how effectively your messages resonate with your audience at each stage.

Data-driven insights are invaluable in refining your approach. Analyze the response rates, conversion rates, and customer feedback to identify areas for improvement. Based on the feedback received, be prepared to adapt your messaging to better address your audience's evolving needs and concerns.

1.5 Embracing Market Research Market research plays a vital role in understanding your audience's preferences, pain points, and aspirations. Through customer surveys, focus groups, and competitor analysis, you can gain valuable insights that shape your marketing strategy.

Take the time to explore your target audience's interests, online behavior, and purchasing patterns. Armed with these insights, you can tailor your marketing messages to resonate more deeply with your prospects, leading to higher engagement and increased conversions.

1.6 Case Study: Personalizing the Journey Let's explore a case study of a company that successfully personalized its marketing journey to match the sophistication levels of its target audience. By analyzing their customer data and understanding the pain points, desires, and motivations of their prospects, they achieved significant improvements in conversion rates and customer retention.

This case study will illustrate how the company used dynamic content, personalized emails, and targeted advertisements to guide prospects through each stage of market awareness. You'll gain valuable insights into how personalization can elevate your marketing efforts and build lasting relationships with your customers.

1.7 Your Action Plan To apply the knowledge gained in this chapter, we encourage you to develop an action plan tailored to your specific business and industry. Consider the following steps:

1. Conduct thorough market research to understand your audience's needs and preferences.
2. Create customer personas that represent the different stages of market awareness.
3. Develop a content strategy that aligns with each stage, addressing the pain points and desires of your target audience.

4. Implement dynamic and personalized content across your marketing channels to deliver a more relevant experience.
5. Monitor the performance of your campaigns and analyze the data to identify areas for improvement.
6. Continuously adapt your messaging based on customer feedback and market trends.

By following this action plan, you'll be well on your way to mastering the art of navigating market sophistication and connecting with your audience in a meaningful way.


**Conclusion**: Understanding the journey of market awareness and adapting your marketing messages accordingly is the foundation of successful online advertising. By tailoring your approach to meet the unique needs of your target audience at each stage, you'll create engaging and effective campaigns that drive explosive sales. In the next chapters, we'll explore additional strategies to enhance your marketing efforts and elevate your online success. So let's continue this exciting journey together, unlocking the full potential of consumer psychology for your business!

# Chapter 2: Building Emotional Connections

Now that you have a solid understanding of market awareness and how to tailor your messages, it's time to delve into the realm of emotions. In Chapter 2, we'll explore the power of emotional connections in driving consumer behaviour and how you can create marketing messages that truly resonate with your audience's heartstrings.

2.1 The Role of Emotions in Decision-Making Emotions play a significant role in the decision-making process. Studies have shown that people often make purchasing decisions based on their feelings rather than solely on rationality. By tapping into the emotional aspect of consumer behaviour, you can create a strong bond with your audience, leading to increased brand loyalty and repeat purchases.

Understanding the different emotions that drive your target audience is crucial. In this section, we'll explore the primary emotions that influence consumer behaviour, such as happiness, fear, love, and curiosity. You'll learn how to evoke these emotions in your marketing messages to create a lasting impact.

2.2 Addressing Desires, Fears, and Frustrations Emotional connections are strengthened when you address your audience's deep desires, fears, and frustrations. People are driven by the desire for pleasure, security, and fulfillment, but they are also guided by the fear of missing out, making the wrong choice, or facing disappointment.

In this section, we'll discuss how to identify and address these desires, fears, and frustrations in your marketing campaigns. By acknowledging and empathizing with your audience's emotional needs, you'll build trust and authenticity, making them more likely to choose your brand over competitors.

2.3 Storytelling that Resonates Storytelling is a powerful tool to create emotional connections with your audience. Through compelling narratives, you can humanize your brand, evoke emotions, and establish a sense of shared experience.

We'll explore the art of storytelling, from crafting engaging brand stories to sharing customer success stories that resonate with your target audience. You'll learn how to use storytelling to evoke emotions, inspire action, and leave a lasting impression on your customers.

2.4 Creating Authenticity and Trust Authenticity and trust are essential elements in building emotional connections with your audience. Consumers are more likely to connect with brands that are genuine, transparent, and aligned with their values.

In this section, we'll delve into strategies to convey authenticity and build trust with your audience. From showcasing behind-the-scenes glimpses of your company to responding to customer feedback with sincerity, you'll discover how to nurture authentic relationships with your customers.

2.5 The Power of User-Generated Content User-generated content (UGC) is a valuable resource for establishing emotional connections. When your customers become brand advocates and share their positive experiences with your products or services, it creates a sense of community and validation.

Learn how to leverage UGC in your marketing efforts, encouraging customers to share their stories, photos, and testimonials. We'll discuss effective ways to showcase UGC across your marketing channels, strengthening emotional connections and social proof.

2.6 Case Study: Eliciting Emotions for Success In this chapter's case study, we'll explore how a brand effectively tapped into emotions to drive their marketing success. Through emotional storytelling, targeted UGC campaigns, and authentic engagement, they created a devoted customer base and witnessed remarkable growth.

This case study will demonstrate the tangible impact of emotional connections on business outcomes and provide actionable insights for your marketing endeavors.

2.7 Your Action Plan Now that you've delved into the world of emotions and their role in consumer behavior, it's time to develop an action plan that leverages emotional connections to enhance your marketing efforts.
Consider the following steps:

1. Conduct research to understand the emotional needs and motivations of your target audience.
2. Develop a content strategy that incorporates emotional storytelling and UGC to connect with your audience on a deeper level.
3. Showcase authenticity and transparency in your brand communication to build trust and loyalty.
4. Encourage customer participation and engagement through UGC campaigns.
5. Monitor the emotional impact of your marketing efforts and analyze the data to refine your strategy.

By applying this action plan, you'll be equipped to build authentic emotional connections with your audience, creating a loyal customer base that drives explosive sales and long-term success.

**Conclusion**: In Chapter 2, we've explored the profound influence of emotions on consumer behavior and how to build emotional connections with your target audience. By understanding and addressing their desires, fears, and frustrations, and incorporating compelling storytelling and authentic engagement, you'll elevate your marketing to a whole new level.

In the next chapter, we'll delve into the process of crafting a unique selling proposition (USP) that sets your brand apart from the competition. So get ready to stand out and leave a lasting impact with your audience as we continue this journey of unlocking online success!

# Chapter 3: The Special Ingredient: Unique Selling Proposition (USP)

In Chapter 3, we'll explore the vital role of a Unique Selling Proposition (USP) in differentiating your brand and capturing the attention of your target audience. Your USP is the special ingredient that sets you apart from your competitors and communicates the unique benefits that only your product or service can offer.

3.1 Defining Your USP Your USP is the essence of what makes your brand and offerings remarkable. It is the concise statement that answers the question, "Why should customers choose you over the competition?" In this section, we'll guide you through the process of defining a compelling USP that aligns with your brand's values and resonates with your target audience.

We'll discuss the key components of a powerful USP, including the specific benefits it provides, the unique features that distinguish your product or service, and the emotional appeal that captures your audience's hearts.

3.2 Identifying Your Competitive Advantage To create a compelling USP, you need to identify your competitive advantage. What makes your brand stand out? Is it your superior quality, exceptional customer service, or innovative technology? Understanding and capitalizing on your strengths will help you craft a USP that is authentic and resonates with your audience.

This section will guide you through analyzing your competitors, identifying gaps in the market, and leveraging your strengths to position your brand uniquely.

3.3 Addressing Customer Pain Points A strong USP addresses the pain points of your target audience and offers a clear solution. By understanding your customers' challenges, you can tailor your USP to demonstrate how your product or service directly addresses their needs and makes their lives better.

In this section, we'll explore ways to conduct customer research and gather insights into your audience's pain points. You'll learn how to craft a USP that speaks directly to the problems your customers face, positioning your brand as the ideal solution.

3.4 Communicating Your USP Effectively Once you've developed your USP, it's essential to communicate it effectively across all your marketing channels. Your USP should be prominently featured in your website, advertisements, social media, and any other customer touchpoints.

We'll discuss strategies for integrating your USP into your marketing materials, ensuring it becomes the central message that resonates with your audience and leaves a lasting impression.

3.5 Case Study: The USP that Changed the Game In this chapter's case study, we'll explore how a brand's unique selling proposition revolutionized their market presence and propelled them to the top of their industry. You'll discover how they crafted a USP that encapsulated their brand's essence and differentiated them from competitors.

This case study will illustrate the transformative impact of a well-defined USP on brand perception and customer loyalty, offering actionable insights for creating your own compelling USP.

3.6 Your Action Plan To harness the power of a Unique Selling Proposition, consider the following steps:

1. Analyze your brand's strengths and identify your competitive advantage.
2. Conduct customer research to understand their pain points and desires.
3. Craft a clear and concise USP that aligns with your brand's values and addresses
4. customer needs.
5. Integrate your USP into all marketing materials and customer touchpoints.
6. Monitor the impact of your USP on customer engagement and conversion rates and adapt as needed.

By following this action plan, you'll leverage your USP to create a distinctive brand identity that captures the attention of your audience and sets the stage for explosive sales and sustainable success.

Conclusion: In Chapter 3, we've explored the significance of a Unique Selling Proposition (USP) in distinguishing your brand and resonating with your target audience. By defining your USP, identifying your competitive advantage, addressing customer pain points, and communicating your USP effectively, you'll position your brand for success.

In the next chapter, we'll unleash your creative brilliance and explore the art of creating a captivating "Big Idea" that grabs your audience's attention and keeps them engaged. So let's continue this exciting journey of unlocking online success, and get ready to elevate your marketing campaigns to new heights!

# Chapter 4: Unleashing Creative Brilliance: "The Big Idea"

In Chapter 4, we'll explore the art of creating a captivating "Big Idea" that sets your marketing campaigns apart from the competition. A "Big Idea" is the creative concept or central theme that underpins your messaging and captures your audience's attention, leaving a memorable impact.

4.1 The Power of "The Big Idea" A compelling "Big Idea" is like a magnet that draws your audience in and keeps them engaged. It's the spark that ignites curiosity, emotions, and action. In this section, we'll delve into the importance of developing a "Big Idea" and how it can elevate your marketing campaigns to new heights.

4.2 Brainstorming and Refining Creative Concepts Generating a "Big Idea" requires creativity and innovation. We'll explore brainstorming techniques to foster creative thinking and unlock fresh perspectives. You'll learn how to engage your team in collaborative ideation sessions, encouraging the flow of innovative concepts.

Once you have a collection of ideas, the refinement process begins. We'll discuss how to evaluate each concept based on alignment with your brand, resonance with your target audience, and feasibility for execution.

4.3 Crafting a Compelling Story A powerful "Big Idea" is often anchored in storytelling. We'll guide you through crafting a compelling narrative that aligns with your "Big Idea" and engages your audience emotionally.
Your story should resonate with your audience's aspirations, fears, and values, and evoke emotions that motivate them to take action. We'll explore storytelling techniques that breathe life into your "Big Idea," making it relatable and unforgettable.

4.4 Consistency Across Marketing Channels To maximize the impact of your "Big Idea," it's crucial to maintain consistency across all marketing channels. Whether it's your website, social media, email campaigns, or advertisements, a cohesive message enhances brand recall and reinforces the emotional connection with your audience.

We'll discuss strategies to integrate your "Big Idea" seamlessly across various channels, ensuring a unified brand experience that resonates with your customers.

4.5 Case Study: The "Big Idea" that Captivated the World In this chapter's case study, we'll explore how a brand's "Big Idea" became a viral sensation, capturing the world's attention and driving unprecedented brand awareness and sales.

Through an engaging and emotionally charged concept, the brand created an unforgettable campaign that touched the hearts of millions. You'll gain valuable insights into the elements that made their "Big Idea" so successful, inspiring you to infuse creativity and innovation into your own marketing campaigns.

4.6 Your Action Plan To harness the power of a captivating "Big Idea," consider the following steps:

1. Initiate brainstorming sessions with your team to generate creative concepts.
2. Evaluate and refine your ideas based on brand alignment and audience resonance.
3. Craft a compelling story that aligns with your "Big Idea" and emotionally connects with your audience.
4. Integrate your "Big Idea" consistently across all marketing channels for maximum impact.
5. Monitor the response to your "Big Idea" and adapt as needed to keep your campaigns fresh and engaging.

By following this action plan, you'll elevate your marketing campaigns with a captivating "Big Idea" that captures the hearts of your audience and sets the stage for remarkable success. Conclusion: In Chapter 4, we've explored the power of a captivating "Big Idea" and how it sets the foundation for extraordinary marketing campaigns. By unleashing your creative brilliance and crafting compelling narratives, you'll captivate your audience and inspire action.

In the next chapter, we'll focus on the art of crafting persuasive copy that complements your "Big Idea" and drives conversions. So let's continue this journey of unlocking online success, and get ready to wield the power of persuasive writing to take your marketing efforts to new heights!

# Chapter 5: The Art of Persuasive Copywriting

In Chapter 5, we'll delve into the art of persuasive copywriting, a critical skill for turning prospects into loyal customers. Crafting compelling and persuasive copy is essential to complement your "Big Idea" and drive conversions. Let's explore the techniques that will make your messages resonate and inspire action.

5.1 Understanding the Psychology of Persuasion Effective copywriting is rooted in an understanding of the psychology of persuasion. We'll explore the principles of persuasion, such as social proof, scarcity, authority, reciprocity, and liking. By incorporating these principles into your copy, you can nudge your audience toward making favorable decisions.

In this section, you'll discover how to leverage psychological triggers to create persuasive messages that resonate with your audience's emotions and motivations.

5.2 Writing Attention-Grabbing Headlines The headline is the first point of contact with your audience. A compelling headline should be attention-grabbing, enticing, and relevant. It's the gateway to your message, and if it fails to captivate, your audience may never read the rest of your content.

We'll explore headline writing techniques that compel your audience to read on, whether it's by promising a benefit, invoking curiosity, or addressing a specific pain point.

5.3 Engaging Storytelling for Connection Storytelling is a potent tool in copywriting. It allows you to create a narrative that resonates with your audience, making your message more relatable and memorable.

We'll delve deeper into storytelling techniques, such as character development, conflict, and resolution. By weaving stories into your copy, you'll forge an emotional connection with your audience, fostering trust and loyalty.

5.4 Addressing Objections and Overcoming Resistance Customers often have objections and hesitations when making purchasing decisions. Addressing these objections in your copy can help ease their concerns and pave the way for conversion.

We'll discuss how to identify common objections and craft persuasive responses that build confidence in your product or service. By pre-emptively addressing concerns, you'll demonstrate your understanding of your customers' needs and position your brand as a trusted advisor.

5.5 Crafting Compelling Calls-to-Action (CTAs) The call-to-action (CTA) is the pivotal moment where you prompt your audience to take the desired action, such as making a purchase, signing up for a newsletter, or contacting you.
We'll explore CTA best practices, from using action-oriented language to creating a sense of urgency. A well-crafted CTA can significantly impact your conversion rates, and we'll provide tips to optimize this crucial element of your copy.

5.6 A/B Testing for Optimization Effective copywriting is an iterative process. A/B testing allows you to compare different variations of your copy to determine which one performs best.

We'll guide you through A/B testing techniques and how to use data to make informed decisions about your copy. By continuously optimizing your messaging, you'll enhance your conversion rates and drive better results.

5.7 Case Study: The Persuasive Copy that Converts In this chapter's case study, we'll explore how a brand's persuasive copywriting strategy transformed their marketing campaigns. You'll gain insights into the language, tone, and psychological triggers that made their copy so effective in driving conversions.

This case study will offer practical lessons that you can apply to your own copywriting efforts, boosting the persuasiveness of your marketing messages.

5.8 Your Action Plan To master the art of persuasive copywriting, consider the following steps:

1. Study the principles of persuasion and apply them to your copy.
2. Craft attention-grabbing headlines that captivate your audience.
3. Incorporate storytelling techniques to create an emotional connection.
4. Address objections and concerns proactively in your copy.
5. Create compelling CTAs that drive action.
6. Implement A/B testing to optimize your copy for better results.

By following this action plan, you'll harness the power of persuasive copywriting and take your marketing campaigns to new heights of success.

**Conclusion**: In Chapter 5, we've explored the art of persuasive copywriting and the psychology behind effective messaging. By understanding the principles of persuasion, crafting attention-grabbing headlines, engaging storytelling, addressing objections, and optimizing your CTAs, you'll create copy that compels your audience to take action.

In the next chapter, we'll dive deeper into the world of consumer psychology and explore how understanding your audience's psychographics can lead to more personalized and impactful marketing messages. So let's continue this journey of unlocking online success, and discover the secrets to connecting with your audience on a personal level!

# Chapter 6: Understanding Psychographics for Personalized Marketing

In Chapter 6, we'll explore the importance of understanding psychographics - the psychological and lifestyle characteristics of your target audience. By delving into their motivations, values, interests, and attitudes, you can create personalized marketing messages that resonate on a deeper, more personal level.

6.1 The Power of Psychographics While demographics provide valuable information about your audience's basic characteristics, psychographics offer insights into their behavior, preferences, and beliefs. Understanding psychographics allows you to connect with your audience on a more emotional and personal level.

In this section, we'll explore the various elements of psychographics and how they influence consumer decisions. You'll learn how to use this information to craft messages that align with your audience's individuality.

6.2 Conducting Customer Surveys and Interviews To uncover the psychographics of your audience, conducting surveys and interviews is essential. By directly engaging with your customers, you can gain firsthand knowledge of their aspirations, values, and lifestyle choices.

We'll discuss effective strategies for creating surveys and conducting interviews that provide valuable psychographic data. Armed with this information, you'll be better equipped to tailor your marketing messages for maximum impact.

6.3 Creating Buyer Personas Buyer personas are fictional representations of your ideal customers, based on psychographic and demographic data. These personas humanize your audience, making it easier to understand and connect with their desires and needs.

In this section, we'll guide you through the process of creating detailed buyer personas. You'll learn how to use these personas to guide your marketing efforts, ensuring that your messages resonate with the right audience segments.

6.4 Segmenting Your Audience Not all customers have the same psychographic profiles. Segmenting your audience based on their shared characteristics allows you to create targeted and personalized marketing campaigns.

We'll explore various segmentation strategies, from behavior-based to interest-based segmentation. By tailoring your messages to specific segments, you can deliver more relevant and impactful content.

6.5 Crafting Personalized Messages Once you have a clear understanding of your audience's psychographics and segmented groups, it's time to craft personalized messages that speak directly to their needs and desires.

In this section, we'll discuss how to create content that addresses the unique preferences of each segment. Personalized messages resonate more deeply with your audience, fostering a sense of connection and understanding.

6.6 Case Study: The Power of Personalization In this chapter's case study, we'll explore how a brand's personalized marketing strategy revolutionized their engagement and conversions. By using psychographic data to create tailored messages, they cultivated brand loyalty and advocacy among their customers.

This case study will showcase the tangible benefits of personalized marketing and offer practical insights for implementing a similar approach in your own campaigns.

6.7 Your Action Plan To leverage psychographics for personalized marketing, consider the following steps:

1. Conduct customer surveys and interviews to gather psychographic data.
2. Create detailed buyer personas that represent your audience segments.
3. Segment your audience based on shared characteristics.
4. Craft personalized messages that speak directly to each segment's preferences and values.
5. Monitor the response to personalized campaigns and analyze data for continuous improvement.

By following this action plan, you'll harness the power of psychographics to create personalized marketing messages that connect deeply with your audience and drive long-term loyalty.

**Conclusion**: In Chapter 6, we've explored the significance of understanding psychographics for personalized marketing. By diving into your audience's motivations, values, interests, and attitudes, you'll be able to create messages that resonate on a personal level.

In the final chapter, we'll unveil the secrets of data-driven marketing and how you can use insights to optimize your strategies, enhance ROI, and make informed decisions for future campaigns. So let's continue this journey of unlocking online success, and discover how data can fuel your marketing success!

# Chapter 7: Unveiling Market Insights: The Secrets of Data-Driven Marketing

In Chapter 7, we'll explore the power of data-driven marketing and how insights derived from data can transform your marketing strategies. Embracing data-driven decision-making allows you to optimize your campaigns, enhance return on investment (ROI), and make informed choices for future marketing endeavors.

7.1 The Role of Data in Marketing Data is the backbone of modern marketing. It provides valuable insights into customer behavior, campaign performance, and market trends. By leveraging data, you can make evidence-based decisions that lead to more effective and efficient marketing efforts.

In this section, we'll delve into the importance of data-driven marketing and how it can revolutionize your approach to reaching and engaging your audience.

7.2 Collecting and Analyzing Data To drive data-driven marketing, you must first collect and analyze relevant data. There are various tools and platforms available to gather data, from website analytics to social media insights and customer surveys.

We'll discuss effective data collection methods and how to use data analysis to uncover meaningful patterns and trends. By understanding your customers' preferences and behaviors, you can tailor your marketing messages for maximum impact.

7.3 Optimizing Marketing Campaigns Data-driven insights allow you to continually optimize your marketing campaigns. By monitoring key performance indicators (KPIs) and analyzing the data, you can identify areas for improvement and make real-time adjustments.

We'll explore A/B testing, conversion rate optimization, and other data-driven optimization strategies that enhance the performance of your campaigns and drive better results.

7.4 Personalization and Segmentation Data-driven marketing enables personalized messaging and effective segmentation. By using data to understand your audience's preferences, you can create content that aligns with their individual interests and needs.

We'll discuss how to use data for dynamic content creation and personalized recommendations, increasing customer engagement and conversions.

7.5 Predictive Analytics Predictive analytics is a powerful tool in data-driven marketing. By analyzing historical data, you can forecast future trends and customer behavior. This valuable foresight allows you to proactively adapt your marketing strategies to stay ahead of the competition.

In this section, we'll explore how to leverage predictive analytics for strategic planning and decision-making.

7.6 Case Study: Data-Driven Marketing Success In this chapter's case study, we'll explore how a brand utilized data-driven marketing to achieve remarkable success. By using data to understand customer preferences, optimize campaigns, and make data-backed decisions, they experienced exponential growth and increased customer loyalty.

This case study will highlight the transformative impact of data-driven marketing and offer practical insights for implementing similar strategies in your own marketing efforts.

7.7 Your Action Plan To embrace data-driven marketing, consider the following steps :

1. Implement data collection tools to gather relevant information about your audience and campaign performance.
2. Analyze data to uncover insights and patterns.
3. Optimize your marketing campaigns based on data-driven insights.
4. Personalize your messaging and content based on customer preferences.
5. Leverage predictive analytics for strategic planning and decision-making.

By following this action plan, you'll harness the power of data-driven marketing to make informed choices, enhance your marketing strategies, and achieve outstanding results.

**Conclusion**: In Chapter 7, we've explored the transformative impact of data-driven marketing. By embracing data and leveraging insights, you can optimize your campaigns, personalize your messaging, and make informed decisions that fuel your marketing success.

# Chapter 8: The Power of Education in Marketing

In Chapter 8, we'll explore the transformative impact of education in marketing. By positioning your brand as a valuable source of knowledge and expertise, you can build trust, authority, and lasting relationships with your audience.

8.1 Becoming an Authority in Your Niche Education-based marketing focuses on providing valuable information and insights to your audience. By sharing your knowledge and expertise, you position your brand as an authority in your niche. This approach not only attracts potential customers but also fosters a sense of credibility and trust.

We'll discuss the various educational content formats, such as blog posts, webinars, tutorials, and ebooks, and how to integrate them into your marketing strategy.

8.2 Engaging and Empowering Your Audience Education-based marketing goes beyond product promotion; it's about empowering your audience with actionable information. By addressing their pain points and offering practical solutions, you can genuinely connect with your customers and add value to their lives.

In this section, we'll explore how to create educational content that engages your audience, fosters interaction, and encourages them to take action.

8.3 Building a Community of Learners Education creates a sense of community among your audience. By fostering a space for learning and discussion, you can create a community of learners who support and learn from each other.

We'll discuss how to build and nurture a thriving online community, where customers feel valued and inspired to engage with your brand.

8.4 Leveraging Webinars and Workshops Webinars and workshops are powerful educational tools that allow you to engage with your audience in real-time. They provide an opportunity to dive deeper into topics, answer questions, and showcase your expertise.
In this section, we'll explore how to plan, promote, and host engaging webinars and workshops that leave a lasting impact on your audience.

8.5 Measuring the Impact of Educational Content Like any marketing strategy, it's essential to measure the impact of your educational content. By tracking key metrics, you can evaluate the effectiveness of your educational initiatives and make data-driven improvements.

We'll discuss the metrics to monitor, such as engagement, conversion rates, and customer feedback, to gauge the success of your education-based marketing.

8.6 Case Study: Educating for Success In this chapter's case study, we'll explore how a brand's education-based marketing strategy transformed their customer relationships and business outcomes. By focusing on providing valuable content and establishing themselves as a thought leader, they achieved remarkable customer loyalty and brand recognition.

This case study will offer practical insights for integrating education into your marketing strategy for lasting success.

8.7 Your Action Plan To harness the power of education in marketing, consider the following steps:

1. Identify key educational topics relevant to your audience.
2 Create valuable educational content in various formats, such as blog posts, webinars, and ebooks.
3. Foster a community of learners and encourage engagement and interaction.
4. Measure the impact of your educational initiatives using relevant metrics.
5. Continuously refine your education-based marketing strategy based on insights.

By following this action plan, you'll establish your brand as a trusted authority and foster lasting relationships with your audience through education.

**Conclusion:** Chapter 8 emphasized the transformative impact of education in marketing. By positioning your brand as a valuable source of knowledge and expertise, you can build trust, authority, and lasting relationships with your audience. Engaging customers with educational content and providing exceptional customer service fosters loyalty and advocacy. By embracing education-based marketing, you empower your audience, create a sense of community, and personalize experiences for maximum impact. As you continue on your marketing journey, remember that education is a powerful tool to connect with your audience and achieve outstanding marketing success. In the following chapter Unveiling Market Insight through Research.. Let's continue this journey of mastery and elevate your marketing strategies to new heights!

# Chapter 9: Unveiling Market Insights through Research

In Chapter 9, we'll delve into the essential role of market research in crafting successful marketing strategies. Market research is the foundation that allows you to gain valuable insights into your target market, enabling you to make data-driven decisions and tailor your marketing efforts for maximum impact.

9.1 The Importance of Market Research Market research provides crucial information about your audience, competitors, and industry trends. By understanding your customers' needs, preferences, and pain points, you can create more targeted and relevant marketing messages.

In this section, we'll explore the significance of market research and its impact on driving effective marketing campaigns.

9.2 Conducting Customer Surveys Customer surveys are a powerful tool for gathering direct feedback from your audience. We'll discuss how to design effective surveys that extract valuable insights about customer satisfaction, product preferences, and brand perception.

By listening to your customers' voices, you can identify areas for improvement and tailor your offerings to meet their needs better.

9.3 Leveraging Focus Groups Focus groups offer an opportunity to engage with a small, representative group of your target audience in a structured discussion. By facilitating open conversations, you can delve deeper into their thoughts, emotions, and perceptions.

We'll explore how to conduct focus groups and analyze the feedback to gain deeper market insights.

9.4 Analyzing Competitor Strategies Understanding your competitors is crucial for positioning your brand effectively. By conducting competitor analysis, you can identify gaps in the market, learn from their successes and failures, and differentiate your offerings.
We'll discuss competitor research techniques and how to use this knowledge to refine your own marketing strategies.

9.5 Exploring Market Trends and Opportunities Market research also involves keeping a pulse on industry trends and emerging opportunities. By staying informed about the latest developments, you can proactively adapt your marketing efforts to stay ahead of the competition.

In this section, we'll explore methods for monitoring market trends and leveraging them to your advantage.

9.6 Case Study: The Power of Market Insights In this chapter's case study, we'll explore how a brand's commitment to market research transformed their marketing approach. By using customer surveys, focus groups, and competitor analysis, they gained a deep understanding of their audience's preferences and pain points.

This case study will highlight the tangible benefits of market research and inspire you to adopt similar research strategies in your marketing campaigns.

9.7 Your Action Plan To harness the power of market research, consider the following steps:

1. Conduct customer surveys to gather direct feedback from your audience.
2. Engage in focus groups to gain deeper insights into customer thoughts and emotions.
3. Analyze your competitors' strategies to identify market opportunities and differentiate your brand.
4. Monitor industry trends and emerging opportunities for proactive adaptation.
5. Use market insights to inform and optimize your marketing strategies.

By following this action plan, you'll empower your marketing efforts with data-driven insights, setting the stage for exceptional success.

**Conclusion**:  market research plays a crucial role in shaping successful marketing strategies. By understanding customer needs, preferences, and market trends, businesses can make informed decisions and create more targeted campaigns. Embracing market research leads to stronger connections with customers and sustained growth in the competitive online advertising landscape. In the next chapter, we'll explore the 80/20 rule's transformative power in optimizing marketing efforts for maximum impact. Let's continue on this journey of mastery and unlock even greater marketing success!

# Chapter 10: The 80/20 Rule: Maximizing Marketing Impact

In Chapter 10, we'll explore the powerful concept of the 80/20 rule, also known as the Pareto Principle, and how it can revolutionize your marketing efforts. By identifying the most impactful 20% of your marketing activities that drive 80% of your results, you can optimize your marketing budget and resources for maximum return on investment.

10.1 Understanding the 80/20 Rule The 80/20 rule states that 80% of outcomes come from 20% of efforts. In the context of marketing, this means that a small portion of your marketing activities yield the majority of your results.

In this section, we'll delve into the principles of the 80/20 rule and its relevance in shaping effective marketing strategies.

10.2 Identifying High-Impact Marketing Activities To apply the 80/20 rule, you must identify the marketing activities that drive the most significant impact on your business. This involves analyzing data, tracking performance metrics, and understanding which strategies resonate most with your audience.

We'll discuss how to use analytics and data-driven insights to pinpoint your high-impact marketing activities.

10.3 Streamlining Resources for Maximum ROI Once you've identified the high-impact activities, the next step is to reallocate your resources to focus on them. By concentrating your efforts on what works best, you can optimize your marketing budget and achieve a higher return on investment.

We'll explore how to streamline resources and prioritize the most effective marketing channels.

10.4 Embracing Continuous Improvement The 80/20 rule is not a one-time fix; it's an ongoing process of refinement and optimization. Continuously monitoring and analyzing your marketing performance allows you to adapt to changing market dynamics and customer preferences.

We'll discuss the importance of embracing continuous improvement in your marketing strategies.

10.5 Real-Life Examples of the 80/20 Rule in Action Real-life examples from successful businesses will illustrate how the 80/20 rule has shaped their marketing success. By learning from their experiences, you can apply the same principles to achieve outstanding results.

10.6 Case Study: The 80/20 Marketing Revolution In this chapter's case study, we'll explore how a brand embraced the 80/20 rule to transform their marketing impact. By identifying their high-impact marketing activities and reallocating resources, they achieved significant improvements in customer engagement and conversions.

This case study will inspire you to adopt a similar approach in your marketing strategies for maximum impact.

10.7 Your Action Plan To leverage the power of the 80/20 rule, consider the following steps:

1. Analyze data and performance metrics to identify high-impact marketing activities.
2. Streamline resources to focus on the most effective marketing channels.
3. Embrace continuous improvement and adapt to changing market dynamics.
4. Learn from real-life examples and apply the 80/20 rule to your marketing strategies.

By following this action plan, you'll optimize your marketing efforts and achieve exceptional results with the 80/20 rule.

**conclusion**: Chapter 10 has uncovered the power of the 80/20 rule in maximizing marketing impact. By identifying the most impactful 20% of marketing activities that drive 80% of results, businesses can optimize their resources for a higher return on investment. Embracing continuous improvement and learning from real-life examples, marketers can refine their strategies to achieve outstanding success. The 80/20 rule serves as a guiding principle for streamlining efforts and focusing on what works best, enabling businesses to stand out in a dynamic and competitive market.

As you apply the 80/20 rule to your marketing endeavors, remember that success is an ongoing journey of mastery and innovation. Embrace change, stay agile, and continue to adapt your strategies to stay ahead in the ever-evolving digital landscape. In the next chapter, we'll recap the key learnings from this ebook and equip you with the tools to unlock online success through mastering consumer psychology and creative brilliance. So, let's forge ahead on this path of marketing excellence and achieve remarkable results in the world of online advertising!

## About the Author

"Darell" - a determined and tenacious individual who turned his struggles in advertising into a journey of success. Throughout his career, Darell faced numerous challenges as he ventured into the competitive world of online advertising. Like many aspiring entrepreneurs, he encountered setbacks, made mistakes, and struggled to sell products and services online.

But instead of being deterred, He embraced his challenges as valuable learning opportunities. He realized that to thrive in the digital landscape, he needed to understand consumer psychology, unleash creative brilliance, leverage data-driven insights, and prioritize customer-centricity. With relentless dedication and a thirst for knowledge, He transformed himself into an excellent advertiser.

Through years of hands-on experience and continuous learning, He mastered the art of online advertising. He developed a deep understanding of consumer behavior and the tactics that resonate with audiences. He uncovered the power of education in marketing and the transformative impact of data-driven strategies.

Fueled by a desire to help others achieve their dreams of success, He decided to pen his experiences, insights, and strategies in a book. "The Unleashed Advertiser: Mastering Explosive Sales Techniques" was born from his passion to empower aspiring online entrepreneurs.

In this book, Darell shares his personal journey of struggle and success, offering valuable lessons and practical guidance for anyone looking to excel in the competitive world of online advertising. He believes that every aspiring entrepreneur has the potential to become an expert in their field by harnessing the power of consumer psychology and creative brilliance.

Through his words, He aims to inspire, educate, and guide readers on their path to online success. He emphasizes the importance of understanding the audience, creating compelling messages, embracing data-driven marketing, and prioritizing customer-centricity. Armed with these insights, Darell believes that readers will unlock the full potential of their online marketing efforts and achieve remarkable results.

As you embark on this journey with Darell, remember that success is not defined by how many times you fall, but by how many times you get back up. Like him, you too can overcome obstacles and thrive in the world of online advertising. So, let's dive into the world of consumer psychology and creative brilliance, and together, let's become experts in the art of online advertising.

**Congratulations on completing** "The Unleashed Advertiser: Mastering Explosive Sales Techniques."

Armed with a comprehensive understanding of consumer psychology, creative brilliance, data-driven insights, and customer-centricity, you now possess the tools to excel in the world of online advertising.

By applying the power of market research, you'll gain valuable insights into your audience and industry, fueling the success of your marketing efforts.

Additionally, the 80/20 rule will revolutionize the way you allocate resources, enabling you to focus on high-impact activities that drive exceptional results.

Remember that success is not a destination; it's a journey of continuous learning, innovation, and improvement. Embrace change, stay agile, and adapt your strategies to stay ahead in the dynamic digital landscape.

Thank you for embarking on this transformative journey with us. May your marketing endeavors be filled with prosperity, growth, and exceptional success.

Best regards,

Darell Cestona
   Author

www.ingramcontent.com/pod-product-compliance
Lightning Source LLC
Chambersburg PA
CBHW080923260726
48661CB00009B/3787